CW01086631

STEP UP TO 10K

STEP UP TO 10K

IMPROVE YOUR 5K TIME AND TRAIN FOR A 10K

ACHIEVE MORE IN RUNNING

JOHN MCDONNELL

First published in 2023 by Greative Books Publishing, Ltd.

Grogey Road

Fivemiletown

Tyrone

BT750NT

Copyright © 2023 by John McDonnell

The moral right of the author has been asserted

All rights reserved.

No part of this book may be reproduced in any form or by any electronic or mechanical means, including information storage and retrieval systems, without written permission from the author, except for the use of brief quotations in a book review.

DISCLAIMER

Keeping physically active is key to maintaining a healthy lifestyle. But it is always best to check with your doctor before taking on a sport like running to ensure it is safe for you to do so. Although this program eases new runners into the sport gently, please ensure you get clearance from your doctor.

PERSONAL 1-TO-1 COACHING

Some runners need that extra little push in order to stay true to their plans. Someone to hold them accountable. Someone to adjust their plans when injuries and niggles start appearing. Someone to answer questions on a daily or weekly basis and explain the ins-and-outs of the training. I work with runners of every ability from the complete beginner to the advanced club runner, all at less than the price of your daily coffee.

Discover a personalized approach to elevate your running journey with my coaching services. Embrace a monthly coaching package featuring comprehensive support: receive weekly training updates, engage in regular video call check-ins, and access unlimited guidance to address all your inquiries and worries. While books and guides provide valuable insights, nothing parallels the impact of individualized coaching. Benefit from tailored training plans geared towards specific races or maintaining peak performance between events.

Moreover, within these coaching packages, you'll discover choices for strength training regimens and personalized meal plans. Running holds transformative power, and these all-encompassing coaching packages aim to sculpt you into the well-rounded athlete you aspire to be. Explore your diverse coaching options today at https://jmruncoach.com/services.

If you are ready to elevate your running and crush new personal records then sign up today. Or you can also reach out to me at John McDonnell Running Coach on Facebook and we can discuss your goals and how I can help you reach them. I am also contactable by email at john@jmruncoach.com.

CHANCE TO WIN A MONTH OF FREE PERSONAL COACHING

I am offering everyone who reads this book an opportunity to win one-month of free one-to-one running coaching. Take a look in the Congratulations Chapter at the end of this book to see how to be in with a good chance of winning and making the most of your new sport.

A SPECIAL INVITATION TO JOIN ACHIEVE ONLINE RUNNING CLUB

I have been the head coach at one running club or another since 2015. It has been an absolute privilege to help runners begin their running lives and to play a part in their improvement in the sport over time. I don't think there is anything more satisfying for a coach than to see athletes achieve their goals. That is why I've started Achieve Running Club, an online running club dedicated to bringing people along in our sport.

This is your personal invitation to join our community, for free, and get the support all runners need. I will be personally moderating the Facebook group and checking in from time to time. All your running related questions answered by like minded and knowledgeable runners. All your running related worries put to rest. Be as active or as quiet as you would like. But it would be great to see photos of your achievements, no matter how big or small you may think they are. Every positive experience is another step into your running life and an inspiration to others following in your footsteps. Even the tough days bring something to the table, so share those as well and I'm sure the rest of the community will benefit.

There will also be a regular newsletter emailed out with tips, advice, discounts, and sharing the successes of our members.

Please get involved. It will help you become the runner you always wanted to be. Use the hashtag #AchieveRC in your social media posts and together let's build this community.

How To Join

Website: https://achieverc.com/join-the-club - When you sign up online you will receive a free printable 8 week running journal in PDF format.

Facebook: facebook.com/groups/achieverc

INTRODUCTION

If you followed my Running for Beginners: The Easiest Guide to Running Your First 5k in Only 6 Weeks, (available at Amazon and other book sellers), and you are looking to build on that, then I'm extremely proud of you. You obviously did well and most importantly, enjoyed the process. Otherwise, you wouldn't be back for more.

If you are picking up this guide without having read the Runners for Beginners book, then we have to start under one of two assumptions. Either you can already run a 5k or you know you have the fitness to run a 5k and want to start at the 10k distance. One way or the other, you would probably benefit from some of the coaching points from the first guide, like breathing techniques, running form and nutrition and hydration tips.

Consider starting there, but if you are happy to skip that and go straight to the 10k, let's do it.

If you are looking to improve your existing 5k time, then this book has a 6 week plan to do just that. I will provide you with all of the training sessions that will enable you to smash through your personal records and give you a foundation to understand a little more about the different types of training and how to make best use of each session.

If you are a 5k runners who would like to move up in distance to the 10k, then this includes a plan for you as well. The good news is that just by moving up in distance, you will also bring your 5k times down. Knocking two birds with one stone is always a great idea, eh? The 10k program is designed to give you all you need to conquer this longer distance with confidence.

CHAPTER 1
ABOUT YOUR COACH

MY NAME IS John McDonnell and I've been a UK Athletics Coach in Running Fitness since 2015. During the past number of years I've worked with countless runners from every level of ability. I have a passion for the sport, and I like nothing better than to see a new runner find that self-belief and go on to achieve their goals, whatever those goals might be. I have great pride in all my runners who continue on in the sport to complete longer distances and go on to take huge satisfaction in their running lives. The sport is incredibly beneficial to me and to the quality of my life. As a matter of fact, the sport saved my life. In my memoir, A Heart for Running, (available on Amazon and other booksellers), you can read about how I suffered a stroke at the age of 48 and how running literally played a key role in getting me back on my feet. I enjoy passing my passion along to my athletes. I hope you find that spark and ignite a love for the sport that I know will encourage a better life for yourself.

How and why did I start running? Well, this is well documented in my book. But to make a long story short, I came home from a vacation to Boston and began looking at some of the photographs we took while away. As it was a summer holiday, most of the photos were of me in shorts and t-shirts. I couldn't believe how over-weight I became. At 5' 10", I weighed 215 lb's. I knew at that point I needed to do something to address my unhealthy lifestyle. I started to do two things. First and foremost, I started making much better food choices. I was eating a lot, and not always the best food or at the right time. I came home from work late, after not eating much during the day, and started eating, more than making up for the missed calories. This needed to change and so it did.

The next thing that needed to change was my lack of physical exercise. I started to make the effort to do some type of exercise every day. It could have been going for a walk, jumping on the stationary bike, or the cross-trainer. Eventually, my wife Roisin and I gave running a try. Here is a paragraph from my memoir that tells a bit of how my early running went:

My first few runs were just awful. I would get to a point about a quarter of a mile away from where I started and just stop. I couldn't go another step and my breathing was out of control. This continued for a few more of these terrible sessions, probably a half dozen attempts. Roisin was getting on far better than I was and this motivated me to keep trying. She found running useful in getting a break from the stresses of work and home life. I wanted to find that inner peace, even if only for a half hour at a time. I had to be missing something. Then one afternoon, on my own, it struck me like a bolt of lightning. What if I slowed down and ran very slow? Would that help? With that one small change, I managed to get beyond that quarter mile and for the first time complete the entire loop without stopping. I was brimming with pride and self-confidence. Roisin and I continued to run this loop together, keeping the pace in check, and before we knew it, we were challenging each other to do a second lap, then a third lap, and eventually a fourth. The day we ran four laps was an incredible experience for both of us. After so many bad runs and progress coming along so remarkably slowly, to put four full loops, over nine miles, behind us was awesome.

These days, I have much more discipline and a healthier lifestyle than I ever had. I've progressed as a runner, as a coach, and as an overall human being and I credit much of my transformation to the sport of running. Starting to run was the single best decision I ever made to improve the quality of my life. My experience, along with my wife, as described above, involved learning on our own. We had no coaching, no guidance on how to breathe, no guidance on our running form. We were just winging it.

You have a great advantage. You will be learning from someone who is not only a qualified coach, but someone who has been there and done it. I started from ground zero and have worked my way up the proverbial ladder. Stick with me through this process and enjoy every accomplishment, both big and small. Every time you run just that one little step further, or that tiny second faster will be cause for celebration.

To learn more about me and follow along with my experiences and personal goals, please have a look at my blog, aheartforrunning.com. I have coaching points, training tips, racing experiences and a whole lot more.

CHAPTER 2
WHY WOULD ANYONE WANT TO RUN 10K

AS A COACH, I strongly recommend running a 10k race for several reasons. It is a challenge that is both achievable and worthwhile on so many levels. Here are some of the top reasons:

Build endurance and aerobic capacity: Running a 10k race requires a certain level of fitness, and training for it can help you build your endurance and aerobic capacity. By gradually increasing your mileage and running longer distances over time, you'll be able to build up your stamina and maintain a faster pace for longer periods of time. This can help you not only during the race but also in other aspects of your life where endurance is important, such as during physical activities or work that requires prolonged physical effort.

Achievable goal: Setting a goal to run a 10k race can be incredibly motivating and give you a sense of purpose. It's a challenging but achievable goal for many runners, regardless of their level of experience or fitness. This can be particularly beneficial for those who may be new to running or who are looking for a new challenge.

Improve overall fitness: Running is a great form of cardiovascular exercise that can help improve your overall fitness. By training for a 10k race, you'll be committing to a regular exercise routine, which can have a positive impact on your health and well-being. This can include benefits such as weight loss, increased energy, improved heart health, and better sleep.

Boost mental health: Running can be a great way to improve your mental health and well-being. Regular exercise has been shown to reduce stress and anxiety, improve mood, and boost self-esteem. Training for and completing a 10k race can give you a sense of accomplishment and pride, which can improve your confidence and self-worth.

Community support: Running can be a social activity that connects you with other runners and provides a sense of community. Training for a 10k race can be an opportunity to meet other runners and share tips, encouragement, and motivation. On race day, the energy and excitement of the crowd can be incredibly motivating and inspiring.

Variety: Running the same route or distance every day can become monotonous, leading to a loss of motivation and interest. Training for a 10k race can add variety to your training routine, as you'll need to mix up your workouts and gradually increase your mileage. This can help keep your workouts interesting and engaging, and prevent burnout.

Personal growth: Setting a goal to run a 10k race can be a way to challenge yourself and push beyond your comfort zone. Training for and completing the race can help you develop mental toughness, discipline, and perseverance, all of which can translate to other areas of your life. Running a 10k race can be an opportunity to push yourself to be your best, both physically and mentally.

Overall, running a 10k race can be an incredibly rewarding experience. With proper training and preparation, it's a challenging but achievable goal that can improve your fitness, mental health, and overall well-being. As a coach, I highly recommend setting your sights on a 10k race and working towards crossing that finish line.

CHAPTER 3
WHAT IT TAKES TO RUN 10K

5K, or 3.1 miles, is a long way to run non-stop. 10k actually feels like much more than twice as far. It isn't, obviously, but it certainly feels like it. However, if you can run 5k, you are not far away from being able to go the extra distance. You can't think of it as two 5k's though. It is an animal all of its own. The key to moving up in distance is to remember the guiding principle from the first book, pace. Run as slow as you need to run in order to cover the distance.

In this book I will be introducing a few different training concepts from the Running for Beginners book. Most importantly, there will be different types of training runs. You will be training to build up the distance as well as adding some additional pace to some of the sessions. This does not mean you will be required to do any sprinting or particularly fast work. Rather you will be asked to change pace on different sessions, instead of running the same pace in every one. So some new concepts will be tempo runs, progression runs as well as intervals.

You will also be introduced to hill sessions as well as the ever-ridiculed, but quite effective, fartlek runs. I will go into more detail on all of these different types of sessions and I know you will enjoy some of them, if not all. As your training varies, so will your improvements. Another added bonus to this type of varied running, is that it will reduce your risk of injury.

More running is required but that said, training to run 10k will not take over your life like marathon training would. You won't be out running for hours on end and requiring days of recovery. You will gradually build in a little more consistency and look to get out for a run four days per week in order to get your weekly miles up. However, this will also require more rest and recovery, which means the addition of easy and recovery runs.

So in a nutshell, jumping up from a 5k to a 10k requires consistency, more and varied training, as well as more recovery time. When we put all of these pieces together, your 10k will fall right into place. In addition, you will find your 5k times plummet. A great result from all of your hard work.

CHAPTER 4
DIFFERENT TYPES OF TRAINING RUNS

AS MENTIONED, I will be introducing some new running concepts in this guide. In the beginner's program you would have had two different parts to your main sessions, running and walking. Now that you've been running the 5k distance, there will be less walking and longer runs. I will be asking you to change pace in some runs and to run on different routes, some with hills. Below are descriptions of the different runs you will be asked to do in these next 6 weeks.

Easy Run

65% of your 5k race pace. This should be what we call "conversation" pace. Basically, this means you can have a fairly comfortable conversation, or at least a few sentences at a time without losing control of your breathing. It is a comfortable pace and you should be able to keep this pace for a good long run.

Fartlek Run

This comes from the Swedish words for speed and play and is popular for training because it offers runners a change of pace during the workout. It is open to interpretation and sessions can differ widely depending on coach and discipline.

Hill Repeats

This is exactly what it sounds like. Running up and down a hill over and over again. This, for some, is difficult and not a lot of fun. However, some runners love them. One way or the other, hill reps are terrific. They provide strength training, speed training, aerobic training all wrapped in one session.

Hilly Run

Unlike hill repeats, a hilly run acts more like real life race conditions. Seldom is found a flat 10k course, so by building in training runs over a hilly course we are working strength, speed and aerobic capacity, just not to the same extent as during a hill repeat session.

. . .

Interval Training

Interval training is normally done on a track, but can be done anywhere that is convenient. These are usually done in sets and repetitions. Traditionally, these are done as say 200m, 400m, 800, 1k, 1 mile repetitions. The aim is to do them all, slightly faster than your normal race pace and have some kind of recovery between each repetition.

There are two different kinds of recovery between intervals, active and static. Active recovery means moving and is either a walk or very slow jog. Static recovery is when you stop moving and get your breathing back down to normal. Please take a moment to download the ARC Target Interval Pace Chart from the Achieve Running Club Website (https://achieverc.com). This chart will explain he pace you should be aiming to run for your intervals of different distances.

Long Slow Run

This is the staple of an endurance athlete's training schedule. There should always be a long slow distance run on the plan. How long and slow will depend on the athlete. For some a long run may be 4 miles, for others it may be 24 miles or more. The key objective is to gradually increase the distance to a point relative to your race distance. How slow? Well it should be at least 2 minutes per mile slower than your 5k race pace, but for newer runners, it may be closer to 1 minute per mile slower. As your race pace gets quicker the slower your relative pace will be on the long runs.

Progression Run

A progression run is one of the more fun training runs as well as one of the more challenging. The objective of a progression run is to run each mile faster than the previous mile. There are no hard and fast rules to this type of session, however, it is best to not go too hard on the first mile as that will make the rest of the miles that much more difficult. You do want it to be a challenge though, so don't make it too easy either.

An example would be a 5 mile progression run with the following splits:

Pace in Kilometers	Pace in Miles
1k: 6:15/k	Mile 1: 10:00/mile
2k: 6:05/k	Mile 2: 9:45/mile
3k: 5:57/k	Mile 3: 9:30/mile
4k: 5:52/k	Mile 4: 9:15/mile
5k: 5:48/k	Mile 5: 9:00/mile
6k: 5:44/k	
7k: 5:40/k	
8k: 5:35/k	

Recovery Run

Recovery runs are scheduled after a difficult session, whether that is a speed session, hill session, or long run. The goal is to help repair the body and decrease the delayed onset muscle soreness, (known as DOMS) that occurs after a tough workout. These types of runs are helpful after any type of physical activity, but for us, it will be after a hard running session. These are run at a comfortable pace, similar to the easy run. The biggest difference between the two is what the goal of the session is. In this case it is recovery and it will follow a hard session.

Steady Run

A steady run is still a good pacy session, it is something to be done as we get further along in our training and we are doing runs over 30 minutes long and up to an hour plus. The pace should be comfortably hard. In other words, between an easy run and a tempo run. Like the name says, the aim will be to keep the pace steady throughout.

Tempo Run

A tempo run is also known as a threshold run. The idea of a tempo run is to target a specific pace and try to hold it for a specified amount of time or distance. As an athlete training for a specific 10k target time, you want to start slow for the first portion of the training run. This is followed by the tempo part where you maintain the faster pace. Then the last part of the run would be back to a slower pace.

An example 5 mile tempo run for a runner looking to target a 55 minute finish time may look like this:

Pace in Kilometers	Pace in Miles
1k: 6:15/k	Mile 1: 10:00/mile
2k: 5:30/k	Mile 2: 8:50/mile
3k: 5:30/k	Mile 3: 8:50/mile
4k: 5:30/k	Mile 4: 8:50/mile
5k: 5:30/k	Mile 5: 10:00/mile
6k: 5:30/k	
7k: 5:30/k	
8k: 6:15/k	

CHAPTER 5
THE BOOK EXPLAINED

THIS GUIDE WILL PROVIDE you with coaching notes at the beginning of each week. These notes will provide a key focus for you to build on as you train. They will explain the concepts of the new types of training runs you will be asked to carry out during that particular week. You will also have some technical points to keep an eye on during that week. If you ever have any questions, please feel free to reach out and contact me on the website or on the Facebook group at Facebook.com/groups/achieverc.

Unlike the Beginners program, you will only do the dynamic warm-ups on the days you are running a hard(er) session. On days when you are running at an easy pace, it is OK to just do your easy warm-up, then start slow and keep it steady. When you are finished with these easier runs, you should do a short 5 minute brisk walk or jog, followed by your post-session static stretching routine.

Every week will consist of 4 training sessions. If, for some reason, you are unable to fit in all 4 days, make a point to skip one of the easy sessions. Although the easy sessions are important, and serve a purpose, they are not as vital to the goals of this program as the harder runs.

CHAPTER 6
FORM AND TECHNIQUE

IN THE FIRST book in this series, Running for Beginners, I gave you quite a few pointers on what running form you should be aiming for. I will reiterate these here:

For running, you want to run tall. This means you want to have a good upright posture. We will work on each of these throughout the eight weeks, but here are the coaching points I'll be looking to introduce to your running form.

- Pretend you have a balloon on a string tied to the base of your skull at the back of your neck, pulling you up from that point - Running Tall

- Shoulders should be relaxed and positioned back and down in relation to your torso
- Imagine you have a bowl of water between your hips and don't want to spill the water from the front or the back
- Your arms should be at 90 degree angles and swing back and forth without crossing in front of your chest
- Your chest should be out forward, opening up your lungs to allow for easier breathing

When it comes to breathing, this is the new runner's biggest complaint. It feels out of control and they feel they have to stop. If this is the case, you need to slow down. Just slow down. That said, in order to help your breathing while running, there are a few things that we can work on.

- Breathe through your mouth **and** your nose. This allows you to get as much oxygen as possible as quickly as possible. You will almost never see a runner, running at effort, with their mouth closed.
- Use a breathing pattern like three strides per breath in and two strides per breath out. This means that each time your foot hits the ground you take a partial breath in or out. There are a

number of advantages to using a breathing technique like this, but for one thing, it reduces the chances of getting a stitch.

- Counting your cadence when you run is really useful. Your cadence is the number of times your feet hit the ground while you are running. It is measured in strides per minute. Counting your cadence while using a breathing pattern, like the one above, takes your mind off the discomfort you may be experiencing. It also gives you a good idea of your pace, much like a metronome would. It makes it much easier to know if you are going faster than normal or if your pace has slackened.

Now that I've covered the basic form and breathing techniques I am going to introduce a couple of new topics; uphill running and downhill running. Both of these are going to eventually be important to you when you run. Once again, there is no magic pill that makes running hills easy, but I can give you some coaching points to help you get up and down efficiently. I'm going to talk about running uphill and downhill but I am making two assumptions. First of all, the hills you are doing are runnable. Some hills just aren't runnable. If they are too steep going up, you may need to put your hands on your thighs and do a power walk. Some hills are too steep going down and are dangerous to run down, particularly for those who haven't been running for years.

The second assumption is that we aren't racing for personal records. There are more advanced hill techniques which I will go over in the next book, but for the purposes of this book, the target is to finish a 10k, not to race it with your eyes out for 6.2 miles. I look forward to teaching you more advanced techniques in the next book in the series, but let's get up these hills and down the other side in one piece.

When it comes to hills, you will find some hill sessions in the plan provided. Try to use these techniques when running those sessions. The more you practice on hills, the better at running them you will be.

Uphill Running

This is one of the most intimidating aspects of running. Some runners report that their heart rate rises when just looking at an upcoming hill. There is no doubt that it takes more effort to go uphill than it does to go down or run on the flat. But here is one of the first key principles on our journey to reaching the 10k distance; running by effort. Running uphill will be slower, but try to keep the same level of effort as you had before you reached the hill. You will have a downhill on the other side to make up for the lost time going up. Just work with the hill, slow down and maintain effort.

The natural tendency will be to lean into the hill, but this will work against you. Especially when leaning from the hips. A slight lean at the ankle joint will be beneficial, but a lean from the hips will make breathing a little bit harder. That is the last thing you want. You want to be able to take in as much oxygen as possible. So remain running tall and keep your chest out and open.

The next thing to work on is shortening your stride. This will come naturally. It is easier to run with good form up a hill as the terrain encourages a shorter stride and a forefoot strike. You will instinctively be landing on your forefoot and recruiting your posterior chain muscles, (glutes, hamstrings and calves), to power up.

Next is to really drive your arms. Here is what I discussed in the Running for Beginners book:

Your arms should be bent at the elbow at a 90 degree angle. They should be driving straight forward and backward. The idea is to not cross over in front of your chest as you run as this closes the chest up and makes it just that little bit harder to breathe. A good visual to keep in mind is to try to use your arms as if you are cross-country skiing and pushing yourself forward as your arm goes back. Another visual you may want to use is to drive your arm back as if you are trying to elbow someone directly behind you (we all want to do that now and again).

As your arms go, so go your legs. If you want to move your legs at a certain pace, you can begin by driving your arms at that pace. It is very difficult to move your arms and legs at a different speed. Try running at a slow pace and move your arms at a fast pace. See, it's very difficult.

When running uphill, your arms are vital to providing momentum. Drive your arms hard and your legs will follow. Keep your arm swing lower, trying not to increase the length of the swing. Rather, a shorter, quicker arm swing will promote shorter and quicker strides.

Uphill running pointers:

- Maintain effort, not speed
- Remain running tall
- Short, powerful arm drive
- Shorter strides
- Landing on your forefoot

Downhill Running

Running downhill certainly sounds a lot more fun than running uphill. I can assure you, 90% of the time this is the case. Keep in mind though, that not everyone runs downhill effectively. There tends to be some people who run well uphill, but not great downhill and the opposite is sometimes true. Having good form and technique running downhill can make a massive difference.

When running downhill, there is more strain on your quadriceps as opposed to running uphill which strains your calves and hamstrings more. So don't be surprised when you start running hills, both up and down, when your legs start aching more. When going downhill, try to let the hill do some of the work for you. It is a great opportunity to get some recovery after going uphill and reaching the peak.

The first thing to do when reaching the top of the hill is reset your breathing. A big blow out and a big breath in. Maybe even two or three of these as you run and start your decline. Next, open up your stride. Longer strides will let the hill do the work for you. Gravity will pull you down the hill as you are in the air for longer. Longer strides will mean a slower leg turnover, and a slightly slower cadence. When you were going up the hill, you were taking shorter strides now you do the opposite.

The next key is to ensure you are well balanced. You may find it easier to hold your arms away from your body just a little to help maintain your balance, much like walking across a 2x4 or a balance beam.

Lastly, try to keep a slight bend in the knee on the leg as it lands. This will lessen the impact on your knees, which will be more important if you are running a lot of hills or if the grade is rather steep.

CHAPTER 7
DYNAMIC EXERCISES

THE DYNAMIC EXERCISES we will be doing will be used to get your relevant muscles warmed up and ready to work. We will be doing these after our initial brisk walk at the start of each session. A demonstration of these dynamic exercises can be viewed on https:// youtube.com/@achieverunningclub.

- Running in place
- High Knees
- Heel Flicks
- Straight Leg Kicks
- A - Skips
- High Skips
- Lunges
- Side Lunges
- Squats

These dynamic exercises should be done after your warm up on your hard sessions. I have included them on the plan when they are necessary. By all means, do them before every run if you wish, but they are only essential prior to your harder sessions.

CHAPTER 8
POST WORKOUT STRETCHING

AFTER EACH WORKOUT, we will be doing some static stretching. When we exercise, our muscles tend to shorten and tense. The purpose of the static stretching will be to return your muscle to the length they were before your session. Each stretch should be held for 15 seconds to be most productive. A demonstration of each of these stretches can be viewed on my YouTube channel at https://youtube.com/@achieverunningclub.

- 3 x Stand tall, reach for the sky, on your toes and hold for 15 seconds
- Spread legs shoulder width apart, fingers interlocked,, bend at the hips, back level reach out in front - hold for 15 seconds
- Reach down intending to touch the ground - hold for 15 seconds

- Walk hands over to right ankle, put both hands around the right ankle - hold for 15 seconds
- Walk hands over to the left ankle, put both hands around the left ankle - hold for 15 seconds
- Slowly move back to the center and slowly raise up
- Put left foot in front of the right, dig both heels into the ground, lean forward on a bent knee - hold for 15 seconds
- Put right foot in front of the left, dig both heels into the ground, lean forward on a bent knee - hold for 15 seconds
- Stand on left leg and hold the right foot in your hand bent at the knee, keep both knees together, push your hips forward - hold for 15 seconds
- Stand on right leg and hold the left foot in your hand bent at the knee, keep both knees together, push your hips forward - hold for 15 seconds
- Hold left arm straight out in front, bring it across your front, pull in with back of right hand - hold for 15 seconds
- Hold right arm straight out in front, bring it across your front, pull in with back of left hand - hold for 15 seconds

- Big circles with arms moving forwards - 15 seconds
- Big circles with arms moving backwards - 15 seconds

As with each part of your sessions, this portion of your workout is important and should never be skipped. It will go a long way to help prevent injuries and reduce lingering soreness.

CHAPTER 9
NUTRITION, HYDRATION & SLEEP

THIS IS a common subject that comes up when starting out with new runners. What do I eat before a run? How soon can I run after I eat? How much water should I drink? Only you will be able to answer these and only after some practice. Generally speaking, it is safe to say that your body should have enough energy stored to run a 5k without consuming a meal beforehand. That may not be the case for a 10k. For a fairly new runner, it is likely you will need some calories to cover the distance, especially if you are running for longer than an hour. You may find it best to consume a light snack about two hours before you run. Something that is not going to upset your stomach and that is fairly quick to digest. Fruit or white carbohydrates of some sort would be ideal as these are digested quickly. If you wish to eat earlier than that, say three hours before running, you would probably eat more complex carbohydrates. But you will need to test your body to see what works best for you.

Some examples of white carbohydrates snacks are:

- White bread (toast) & Jam
- White rice
- Potatoes
- Cereal

Some examples of complex carbohydrates foods include:

- Wheat or wholemeal bread
- Brown rice
- Sweet potatoes
- Rolled Oats (Oatmeal)

As for water, it is best practice to be fairly well hydrated all day, every day. As a minimum, one liter of water per day should be consumed. If you are running in a warm climate, then you should be drinking more. Always bring water with you when you are training so that you can drink at least 500ml after each session. A good practice, particularly in a warm climate where dehydration is more of a risk, is to weigh yourself before a session and weigh yourself after a session. Whatever the difference should be made up by drinking water, as that is what makes up the weight lost during your workout.

After a training session you should aim to get a meal including a good mix of protein, carbohydrates and fats. Too many people neglect to get enough protein in their diet. When you are involved in an exercise program, like this one, it is so important to consume protein. This is what your body uses to build back the muscle fibers after the challenges you are giving them during your workout. The common guidance is to get these proteins, carbs and fats as soon after your workout as you can. Within an hour or sooner if possible.

Taking up a new sport is exciting, but it is also a great time to make positive changes to your lifestyle. This is a terrific opportunity to address any sleep issues you may have. Running is a great sport to help anyone get their sleep regime on track. Your body will make much better gains from the exercise you perform if you give it ample rest and time to rebuild your muscles. Running promotes a healthy sleep cycle, so do your best to take advantage of the effort you are putting in.

You will find nutritional advice and recipes at https://achieverc.com/recipes-for-runners.

CHAPTER 10
HOW SHOULD IT FEEL

YOU WILL HAVE good days and bad days. Every single runner on the planet will tell you that. Some days it feels easy and other days it feels hard. Don't be discouraged when you have a bad session. Give yourself a pat on the back for doing your best and getting through it. Tell yourself that the next one will be better, because it most likely will.

As you increase your time on your feet, as well as your distance, you will find that some days are better than others. On those long runs when you are covering longer distances than you have ever done, you will find your legs will want to seize up. If you drive somewhere to run a five or six mile run and then drive home again, you may find it hard to lift your legs out of the car. This is fairly normal. You are definitely making gigantic strides forward when this is happening. It's not a bad sign whatsoever. Unless it is sharp, acute pain, in which case you should seek medical attention. Otherwise, maybe a few painkillers and you will be fine. This is when you will find the recovery runs that are on the schedule far more important. You may not want to run on sore, tired legs, but the recovery run is there to ensure you aren't laid up for four or five days with DOMS.

On these long slow distance runs, you should still be running at conversation pace. This means that it should feel like you can talk with a running partner, if you have one. These are the runs when a partner can be much more enjoyable. The miles and the minutes just tick over when you have some good company.

What to do if you experience pain

As runners, we all experience soreness. This is normal, especially if you are new to the sport. You are using muscles and moving in ways that many of you haven't used or done in a long time, if ever. This is where you must take extra time to stretch as per the program. If you have time, you should stretch, as often as you can, not just immediately after your running sessions. If you can squeeze in 10 minutes in the morning, or before bed, that would go a long way to helping with the soreness.

It is not uncommon for new runners to experience knee pain, calf pain or sore glutes after a few weeks. Most of the time this can be remedied with straight forward stretching. Sometimes this isn't enough, and you may want to have a foam roller at the ready. Just like stretching, foam-rolling can be done daily and will also be a substantial help. This is the case even if you aren't experiencing soreness or pain. If you can fit in a regular foam rolling session, you may be able to prevent the discomfort in the first place.

If, however, you are experiencing any sharp, acute pains or if you have some sort of "event" while running, it will be best to see a sports massage therapist, a physiotherapist, or even a doctor, to see if they can offer some assistance. By event, I mean you twist an ankle and hear a pop or crack. Perhaps you experienced a fall and bang your head and feel light headed or woozy. These are examples of when you may want to seek more immediate medical assistance. Most of the time, and I do mean most of the time, the pain experienced by a new runner is temporary, and by continuing to run, stretch and foam roll your body will adapt and get used to this new exercise. The point is to not panic if you are experiencing non-traumatic pain.

As you increase the distance and time you are running as well as covering more weekly miles, it is a good idea to get in touch with a sports massage therapist. They will be a major help in alleviating some of your lingering pain and also help prevent overuse injuries. Don't be fooled by the term massage though. A sports massage is anything but relaxing. They can be uncomfortable, but better to be uncomfortable in the hands of a professional than to be injured just when you are making such excellent progress with your running. During the course of this six week 10k program I would suggest at least one and preferably two sports massages during your training plan.

You can see some examples of foam rolling on my youtube channel, https://youtube.com/@achieverun ningclub

CHAPTER 11
6 WEEK PLAN - FINISHING YOUR FIRST 10K

THIS 6 WEEK plan will work on a number of principles. First you will be gradually building up your weekly long run. In the Beginner's 5k program, we did all of the sessions based around time, for example, *run for 30 minutes*. In this program, we will be running by distance. This is a tried and true method of improving your fitness, stamina and believe it or not, your strength and speed. Secondly, I will be building your weekly miles up each week from the first week through week 6. This won't be the case every week, but definitely from where you start to where you finish will be an increase.

I will be giving you some easy sessions each week and some harder sessions. You will never get two hard sessions back to back. You will get easy weeks, hard weeks and some in between. You will never get two hard weeks back to back. These are some of the fundamentals that this program will follow. Each week will consist of four training days and I will include some of the keys for that week in the *Coaching Notes* at the beginning of the week. As always, if you have any questions, please feel free to reach out to me on my website https://achieverc.com/10k-plan-feedback.

I ask you to go out and try to give each session your best effort. If it is a slow run, you should run slow. If it is a hard session you should give it more effort. There doesn't necessarily need to be a huge difference in your hard effort and your easy effort, but there should be a difference.

Unlike my Running for Beginners book, where I cover coaching points and tips on how to begin running, this program will focus on the different types of training that will be involved. However, don't neglect all the coaching points from the beginners book. These are the foundations for your running and will carry through into the future. Make sure to use the breathing techniques, running form tips, and any of the notes you've logged from that first leg of your running career. Once again, I suggest keeping a running journal to note how your training is going and what is working and what isn't working for you personally.

Each week there will be four sessions. They should be done in the order in which they are listed, however, it will be up to you what days suit you best. Try to get the recovery runs done the day immediately after the session before. This will help get you ready for the rest of the week and aid in your muscle recovery.

One other thing you may notice is that I am not asking you to do the dynamic warm up before all of the sessions. The only days you will be doing the dynamic warmups are on the days when you see them on the plan. You will still be doing the post workout stretching and I still recommend yoga and stretching whenever you can, even on the days you don't run. The more often you do a few minutes of stretching the better.

The 24 sessions will be a challenge, but nobody progresses in the sport of running because it is easy. We get better because we love being challenged. We love facing up to the hard work because we know, when it is done, the result will be so worthwhile.

In this case, you may try to visualize crossing the finish line at your first 10k. See yourself doing so with a huge smile on your face, brimming with pride. You have done what you set out to do. You have proven to yourself and everyone you know that you are capable. You are stronger than anyone thought. You have stamina, courage, and commitment. Running for 10 kilometres (6.2 miles) is a massive accomplishment. Let's get started and write your story as a 10k runner!

CHAPTER 12
WEEK 1

COACHING NOTES

This first week will include a steady run, an interval session, a recovery run and a long slow run. All of these are described in Chapter 2: Different Types of Training Runs. A couple of things to keep in mind. First of all, the interval session is an introduction to running faster. This is *not* a sprint session. We are endurance runners, not sprinters. Not to mention, 800m is a long way to run at a faster pace. So keep it comfortably hard on your first interval session.

As for the long slow distance run, this is meant to be slower than an easy run. It should feel comfortable the whole way around. It doesn't matter what your pace is on this run as long as it is slow and you cover the distance. On these gentler paced sessions, it is a great idea to really focus on your running form. Good form should be a habit now, but it is beneficial to check in now and again to ensure you are making it as easy as possible for yourself.

Remember the running cues from the beginners program:

- Run tall
- Chest out
- Shoulders back and down
- Relaxed
- Arms at 90 degrees and carried low

Session 1 (Day 1) - Steady Run
  Warm-up
  Slow jog - 5 minutes
  Main Session
  3 miles steady run
  Cool-Down
  Slow jog - 5 minutes
  Stretching Routine
  As described in the Post Workout Stretching

Session 2 (Day 2) - Interval Session
  Warm-up

Slow jog - 5 minutes
Dynamic Warm-up

- Running in place - 20 seconds
- High Knees - 20 seconds
- Running in place - 20 seconds
- Heel flicks - 20 seconds
- Running in place - 20 seconds
- Straight Leg Kicks - 20 seconds
- Running in place - 20 seconds
- A - Skips - 20 seconds
- Running in place - 20 seconds
- Lunges - 10 (5 each leg)
- Running in place - 20 seconds

Main Session

2 x 800m repeats (approx. ½ mile) with 60 seconds
static recovery between each rep. **Static recovery
means standing still, long, slow, deep breaths**

2 minute static recovery

2 x 800m repeats (approx. ½ mile) with 60 seconds
static recovery between each rep

Cool-Down

Slow jog - 5 minutes

Stretching Routine

As described in the Post Workout Stretching

Session 3 (Day 3) - Recovery Run

Warm-up

Slow jog - 5 minutes

Main Session

3 mile (5k) recovery run

Cool-Down

Slow jog - 5 minutes

Stretching Routine

As described in the Post Workout Stretching

Session 4 (Day 4) - Long Slow Distance Run

Main Session

3.5 miles (approx. 6k) long slow run

Stretching Routine

As described in the Post Workout Stretching

CHAPTER 13
WEEK 2

COACHING NOTES

Well done getting through week 1. You had a few different types of sessions introduced to you and now in the second week I will be giving you some additional types of work. This week has an easy run, a hilly run, another easy run, and a long slow distance run. The majority of the work this week is slow. Don't try to over-work your slow runs. Focus on good form and your breathing techniques.

Session 1 (Day 5) - Easy Run

Main Session

3 miles easy run

Stretching Routine

As described in the Post Workout Stretching

. . .

Session 2 (Day 6) - Hilly Run

Warm-up

Slow jog - 5 minutes

Dynamic Warm-up

- Running in place - 20 seconds
- High Knees - 20 seconds
- Running in place - 20 seconds
- Heel flicks - 20 seconds
- Running in place - 20 seconds
- Straight Leg Kicks - 20 seconds
- Running in place - 20 seconds
- A - Skips - 20 seconds
- Running in place - 20 seconds
- Lunges - 10 (5 each leg)
- Running in place - 20 seconds

Main Session

3 miles (5k) hilly run

Cool-Down

Slow jog - 5 minutes

Stretching Routine

As described in the Post Workout Stretching

. . .

Session 3 (Day 7) - Easy Run

Main Session

3 mile (5k) easy run

Stretching Routine

As described in the Post Workout Stretching

Session 4 (Day 8) - Long Slow Distance Run

Main Session

4 miles (approx. 6.5k) long slow run

Stretching Routine

As described in the Post Workout Stretching

CHAPTER 14
WEEK 3

COACHING NOTES

Week 3 is here already and you haven't even broken a sweat! OK, that may be untrue, but you are well on your way to reaching your goal. Well done to you. This week you will be introduced to hill repeats. I know, they sound like great fun. If you can learn to like the hills you will make huge improvements quickly. Hills are speed work, strength work and aerobic work in disguise and all wrapped up in one. You will love the challenge running them will bring. Read the technical aspects of running both uphill and downhill in the chapter called Form & Technique.

Session 1 (Day 5) - Easy Run

Main Session

3 miles easy run

Stretching Routine

As described in the Post Workout Stretching

Session 2 (Day 6) - Hill Repeats

Warm-up

Slow jog - 5 minutes

Dynamic Warm-up

- Running in place - 20 seconds
- High Knees - 20 seconds
- Running in place - 20 seconds
- Heel flicks - 20 seconds
- Running in place - 20 seconds
- Straight Leg Kicks - 20 seconds
- Running in place - 20 seconds
- A - Skips - 20 seconds
- Running in place - 20 seconds
- Lunges - 10 (5 each leg)
- Running in place - 20 seconds

Main Session

Choose a hill that is steep enough that it will challenge you. It should be long enough to enable you to climb up for at least 60 seconds.

3 sets of 3 x 30 second repeats uphill with a slow jog down for recovery. When you reach the bottom of the hill, turn and run back up the hill straight away.

Take 2 minutes recovery between each set of 3 repeats
1 set of 2 x 60 seconds repeats uphill with a slow jog down for recovery. When you reach the bottom of the hill after the first one, turn and run back up the hill straight away for the last rep.

Cool-Down
Slow jog - 15 minutes
Stretching Routine
As described in the Post Workout Stretching

Session 3 (Day 7) - Recovery Run
  Main Session
  3 mile (5k) recovery run
  Stretching Routine
  As described in the Post Workout Stretching

. . .

Session 4 (Day 8) - Long Slow Distance Run

Main Session

4.5 miles (approx. 7k) long slow run

Stretching Routine

As described in the Post Workout Stretching

CHAPTER 15
WEEK 4

COACHING NOTES

You are doing fantastic. I'm really pleased to see you here at the beginning of week 4. You have been doing some really interesting and varied running. I hope you are enjoying the progress you are making. It may be hard to see it while you are in the middle of the training, but you are most definitely progressing. That is why it is important to trust the plan, have faith in yourself and know that at the end of these 6 weeks, you will be in great shape and running better than ever.

This week you will be doing your first tempo run. This is going to add some pace into your mid-week run, but without the recovery period you got during the interval session. Tempo runs are a terrific way to make progress in your running and I know you will do well with this one.

. . .

Session 1 (Day 9) - Easy Run

Main Session

3 miles easy run

Stretching Routine

As described in the Post Workout Stretching

Session 2 (Day 10) - Tempo Run

Warm-up

Slow jog - 5 minutes

Dynamic Warm-up

- Running in place - 20 seconds
- High Knees - 20 seconds
- Running in place - 20 seconds
- Heel flicks - 20 seconds
- Running in place - 20 seconds
- Straight Leg Kicks - 20 seconds
- Running in place - 20 seconds
- A - Skips - 20 seconds
- Running in place - 20 seconds
- Lunges - 10 (5 each leg)
- Running in place - 20 seconds

Main Session

3 mile (5k) tempo run

- Mile 1: easy
- Mile 2: pick up the pace to be uncomfortably hard, but obviously not a sprint. The pace should be your recent pace for a 5k. Download the target interval training pace chart by visiting: https://achieverc.com/
- Mile 3: easy

If you work in k's

- K1: easy
- K2: easy
- K3: pick up the pace to be uncomfortably hard, but obviously not a sprint. The pace should be your recent pace for a 5k.
- K4: hold the pace from K3
- K5: easy

Cool-Down
Slow jog - 5 minutes
Stretching Routine
As described in the Post Workout Stretching

Session 3 (Day 11) - Steady Run

Main Session

3 mile (5k) Steady run

Stretching Routine

As described in the Post Workout Stretching

Session 4 (Day 12) - Long Slow Distance Run

Main Session

5 miles (approx. 8k) long slow run

Stretching Routine

As described in the Post Workout Stretching

CHAPTER 16
WEEK 5

COACHING NOTES

Week 5 already! Super job reaching this point. You will be hitting most of your goals by now, but please do keep with the program. You should be keeping to your plan and making sure that your easy and slow runs are easy and slow. Those sessions that require hard work should give you a huge sense of satisfaction when completed. Give yourself serious kudos for putting in all the work to get this far.

This week will include one of my personal favorites, the progression run. The key to this run is to ensure that each mile, (or kilometre) you run is a little faster than the previous one. Hint: don't start too quickly or you make it really hard on yourself.

Please do consider posting your progress and share

your experiences on our Facebook group. It is a great place for support and encouragement.

Session 1 (Day 13) - Easy Run
  Main Session
  3 miles easy run
  Stretching Routine
  As described in the Post Workout Stretching

Session 2 (Day 14) - Progression Run
  Warm-up
  Slow jog - 5 minutes
  Dynamic Warm-up

- Running in place - 20 seconds
- High Knees - 20 seconds
- Running in place - 20 seconds
- Heel flicks - 20 seconds
- Running in place - 20 seconds
- Straight Leg Kicks - 20 seconds
- Running in place - 20 seconds
- A - Skips - 20 seconds
- Running in place - 20 seconds
- Lunges - 10 (5 each leg)
- Running in place - 20 seconds

Main Session

4 mile (6.5k) Progression run

Each mile, (or kilometre) quicker than the previous one

Cool-Down

Slow jog - 5 minutes

Stretching Routine

As described in the Post Workout Stretching

Session 3 (Day 15) - Easy Run

Main Session

3 mile (5k) Steady run

Stretching Routine

As described in the Post Workout Stretching

Session 4 (Day 16) - Long Slow Distance Run

Main Session

5.5 miles (approx. 10k) long slow run

Stretching Routine

As described in the Post Workout Stretching

CHAPTER 17
WEEK 6

COACHING NOTES

This is it. You are nearly there. You've not only just about reached your 10k distance, but you've made significant improvements in your running. I'm extremely proud of you for taking on this challenge. You've done amazing and I really hope you have joined and posted up your progress on the facebook group.

Session 1 (Day 7) - Easy Run
    Main Session
    4 miles easy run
    Stretching Routine
    As described in the Post Workout Stretching

· · ·

Session 2 (Day 18) - Fartlek Run
Warm-up
Slow jog - 5 minutes
Dynamic Warm-up

- Running in place - 20 seconds
- High Knees - 20 seconds
- Running in place - 20 seconds
- Heel flicks - 20 seconds
- Running in place - 20 seconds
- Straight Leg Kicks - 20 seconds
- Running in place - 20 seconds
- A - Skips - 20 seconds
- Running in place - 20 seconds
- Lunges - 10 (5 each leg)
- Running in place - 20 seconds

Main Session

3 mile fartlek run, alternating every other minute on (pick up the pace) and every other minute off (slow down the pace). This is a fun session and one you should really enjoy by adding the speed work into a normal 3 mile run.

Cool-Down
Slow jog - 5 minutes

Stretching Routine

As described in the Post Workout Stretching

Session 3 (Day 19) - Easy Run

    Main Session

    3 mile (5k) Steady run

    Stretching Routine

    As described in the Post Workout Stretching

Session 4 (Day 20) - Long Slow Distance Run - 10k Day!!!

    Main Session

    6.2 miles (approx. 10k) long slow run

    Stretching Routine

    As described in the Post Workout Stretching

CHAPTER 18
5K FOCUSSED IMPROVEMENT

FOR SOME OF YOU, 5k is plenty. You've managed to run the distance, you may love the challenge running a 5k brings. It is a challenge for sure. Instead of moving up to the 10k distance, perhaps you are more inclined to stick at the 5k distance and wish to improve your time. There are many reasons why this may be the case. For example, maybe you haven't got the time to dedicate over an hour to your long runs. Maybe you want to challenge yourself to a specific target 5k time before moving up in distance. Or perhaps you've already done the 10k and want to focus on improving your 5k time. Whatever the reason, this is the perfect 5k program to improve your time.

The philosophy behind this plan is to do a little more speed work than in the 10k plan. You will still be increasing your weekly miles and a little bit on your long run, just not all the way up to 10k. This also has 4 training days per week. You have 6 weeks to make this improvement. It would be a really good idea to run a 5k as fast as you can before you start this program and use it as a benchmark. I'd be very interested to hear how much you improved your time after the 6 weeks is up. Please reach out and let me know your results, before and after. You can do this at https://achieverc.com/5k-improve ment-plan-feedback.

CHAPTER 19
WEEK 1

COACHING NOTES

This first week will include a steady run, an interval session, a recovery run and a long slow run. All of these are described in Chapter 2: Different Types of Training Runs. A couple of things to keep in mind. First of all, the interval session is an introduction to running faster. This is *not* a sprint session. We are endurance runners, not sprinters. Not to mention, 400m is a long way to run at a faster pace. So keep it comfortably hard on your first interval session. The aim should be to run each rep at the same pace.

As for the long slow distance run, this is meant to be slower than an easy run. It should feel comfortable the whole way around. It doesn't matter what your pace is on this run as long as it is slow and you cover the distance. On these gentler paced sessions it is a great idea to really focus on your running form. Good form should be a habit now but it is beneficial to check in now and again to ensure you are making it as easy as possible for yourself.

Remember the running cues from the beginners program:

- Run tall
- Chest out
- Shoulders back and down
- Relaxed
- Arms at 90 degrees and carried low

Session 1 (Day 1) - Steady Run
Warm-up
Slow jog - 5 minutes
Main Session
3 miles steady run
Cool-Down
Slow jog - 5 minutes
Stretching Routine
As described in the Post Workout Stretching

Session 2 (Day 2) - Interval Session

Warm-up
Slow jog - 5 minutes
Dynamic Warm-up

- Running in place - 20 seconds
- High Knees - 20 seconds
- Running in place - 20 seconds
- Heel flicks - 20 seconds
- Running in place - 20 seconds
- Straight Leg Kicks - 20 seconds
- Running in place - 20 seconds
- A - Skips - 20 seconds
- Running in place - 20 seconds
- Lunges - 10 (5 each leg)
- Running in place - 20 seconds

Main Session

4 x 400m repeats (approx. 1/4 mile) with 60 seconds static recovery between each rep. **Static recovery means standing still, long, slow, deep breaths**

2 minute static recovery

4 x 400m repeats (approx. 1/4 mile) with 60 seconds static recovery between each rep

The 400m reps should be run at slightly faster than your target 5k pace (look at the pace chart you downloaded earlier).

Cool-Down
Slow jog - 5 minutes
Stretching Routine
As described in the Post Workout Stretching

Session 3 (Day 3) - Recovery Run
Warm-up
Slow jog - 5 minutes
Main Session
3 mile (5k) recovery run
Cool-Down
Slow jog - 5 minutes
Stretching Routine
As described in the Post Workout Stretching

Session 4 (Day 4) - Long Slow Distance Run
Main Session
3.5 miles (approx. 6k) long slow run
Stretching Routine
As described in the Post Workout Stretching

CHAPTER 20
WEEK 2

COACHING NOTES

Well done getting through week 1. This week you have another interval session, this time 800m repeats. These are tough ones, but the focus should be to, once again, finish each of them at the same pace. Try not to go out and do the first one too fast and suffer through the remaining 5 reps slower than the first.

You also have a hilly run to take on. This isn't a hill session, just ensure you run a route that has a good few hills on it that will push your breathing and challenge you. Make sure to follow the tips from earlier in the book on uphill and downhill running.

Session 1 (Day 5) - Easy Run
   Main Session

3 miles easy run

Stretching Routine

As described in the Post Workout Stretching

Session 2 (Day 6) - Interval Session

Warm-up

Slow jog - 5 minutes

Dynamic Warm-up

- Running in place - 20 seconds
- High Knees - 20 seconds
- Running in place - 20 seconds
- Heel flicks - 20 seconds
- Running in place - 20 seconds
- Straight Leg Kicks - 20 seconds
- Running in place - 20 seconds
- A - Skips - 20 seconds
- Running in place - 20 seconds
- Lunges - 10 (5 each leg)
- Running in place - 20 seconds

Main Session

3 x 800m repeats (approx. 1/2 mile) with 60 seconds static recovery between each rep
2 minute static recovery (standing still, long, slow,

deep breaths)

3 x 800m repeats (approx. ½ mile) with 60 seconds static recovery between each rep

The 800m reps should be run at slightly faster than your target 5k pace (look at the pace chart you downloaded earlier).

Cool-Down

Slow jog - 5 minutes

Stretching Routine

As described in the Post Workout Stretching

Session 3 (Day 7) - Recovery Run

Main Session

3 mile (5k) Recovery run

Stretching Routine

As described in the Post Workout Stretching

Session 4 (Day 8) - Hilly Run

Main Session

3 miles (approx. 5k) long slow run

Stretching Routine

As described in the Post Workout Stretching

CHAPTER 21

WEEK 3

COACHING NOTES

Here we are at week 3 already. Well done on getting through the first two weeks in one piece. You are doing great so keep up the hard work. This week sees your first hill repeat session. The sooner you get used to the hills, the quicker your times will come down. If you can focus on good uphill and downhill technique, you will make the hills just that little bit easier.

You are also getting your longest run of the program so stay focussed and get through this week, you have got this!

Session 1 (Day 5) - Easy Run
Main Session
3 miles easy run

Stretching Routine

As described in the Post Workout Stretching

Session 2 (Day 6) - Hill Repeats

Warm-up

Slow jog - 5 minutes

Dynamic Warm-up

- Running in place - 20 seconds
- High Knees - 20 seconds
- Running in place - 20 seconds
- Heel flicks - 20 seconds
- Running in place - 20 seconds
- Straight Leg Kicks - 20 seconds
- Running in place - 20 seconds
- A - Skips - 20 seconds
- Running in place - 20 seconds
- Lunges - 10 (5 each leg)
- Running in place - 20 seconds

Main Session

Choose a hill that is steep enough that it will challenge you. It should be long enough to enable you to climb up for at least 60 seconds.

3 sets of 4 x 30 second repeats uphill with a slow jog down for recovery

Take 2 minutes recovery between each set of 3 repeats

1 set of 4 x 60 seconds repeats uphill with a slow jog down for recovery

Cool-Down

Slow jog - 15 minutes

Stretching Routine

As described in the Post Workout Stretching

Session 3 (Day 7) - Recovery Run

Main Session

3 mile (5k) recovery run

Stretching Routine

As described in the Post Workout Stretching

Session 4 (Day 8) - Long Slow Distance Run

Main Session

4 miles (approx. 7k) long slow run

Stretching Routine

As described in the Post Workout Stretching

CHAPTER 22

WEEK 4

COACHING NOTES

Week 4 will see you doing your first tempo run. A tempo run will give you something close to your 5k experience for the middle miles. Work hard on this run and know how beneficial it will be on race day. So this week it is another easy run, a tempo run, a recovery run and another hilly run. Nail these sessions and you've got a lot of the hard work done.

Session 1 (Day 9) - Easy Run

Main Session

3 miles easy run

Stretching Routine

As described in the Post Workout Stretching

. . .

Session 2 (Day 10) - Tempo Run

Warm-up

Slow jog - 5 minutes

Dynamic Warm-up

- Running in place - 20 seconds
- High Knees - 20 seconds
- Running in place - 20 seconds
- Heel flicks - 20 seconds
- Running in place - 20 seconds
- Straight Leg Kicks - 20 seconds
- Running in place - 20 seconds
- A - Skips - 20 seconds
- Running in place - 20 seconds
- Lunges - 10 (5 each leg)
- Running in place - 20 seconds

Main Session

3 mile (5k) tempo run

- Mile 1: easy
- Mile 2: pick up the pace to be uncomfortably hard, but obviously not a sprint. The pace should be your target pace for a 5k. See the pace chart you downloaded earlier.
- Mile 3: easy

If you work in k's

- K1: easy
- K2: easy
- K3: pick up the pace to be uncomfortably hard, but obviously not a sprint. The pace should be your target pace for a 5k. See the pace chart you downloaded earlier.
- K4: hold the pace from K3
- K5: easy

Cool-Down

Slow jog - 5 minutes

Stretching Routine

As described in the Post Workout Stretching

Session 3 (Day 11) - Recovery Run

Main Session

3 mile (5k) Steady run

Stretching Routine

As described in the Post Workout Stretching

Session 4 (Day 12) - Hilly Run

Main Session

4 miles (approx. 6.5k) hilly run

Stretching Routine

As described in the Post Workout Stretching

CHAPTER 23
WEEK 5

COACHING NOTES

Wow, you have four weeks done. Amazing! I'm really pleased for you and hopefully you are finding this training experience fulfilling. I know you certainly will when you tackle your target 5k and see your finish time plummet. This week, we return to the intervals with 1k repeats. These are probably the most beneficial sessions you will have for targeting a fast 5k race. So, once again, try your best to run each one at a consistent pace according to the chart you downloaded from https://achieverc.com/.

In addition to the interval session you also have an easy run, a recovery run and another long slow distance run.

. . .

Session 1 (Day 13) - Easy Run

Main Session

3 miles easy run

Stretching Routine

As described in the Post Workout Stretching

Session 2 (Day 14) - Interval Session

Warm-up

Slow jog - 5 minutes

Dynamic Warm-up

- Running in place - 20 seconds
- High Knees - 20 seconds
- Running in place - 20 seconds
- Heel flicks - 20 seconds
- Running in place - 20 seconds
- Straight Leg Kicks - 20 seconds
- Running in place - 20 seconds
- A - Skips - 20 seconds
- Running in place - 20 seconds
- Lunges - 10 (5 each leg)
- Running in place - 20 seconds

Main Session

2 x 1k repeats with 60 seconds static recovery between each rep. **Static recovery means standing still, long, slow, deep breaths**

2 minute static recovery

2 x 1k repeats with 60 seconds static recovery between each rep

Each 1k rep should be run at slightly faster than your target 5k pace (look at the pace chart you downloaded earlier).

Cool-Down
Slow jog - 5 minutes
Stretching Routine
As described in the Post Workout Stretching

Session 3 (Day 15) - Recovery Run
    Main Session
    3 mile (5k) Recovery run
    Stretching Routine
    As described in the Post Workout Stretching

· · ·

Session 4 (Day 16) - Long Slow Distance Run

Main Session

4.5 miles (approx. 7k) long slow run

Stretching Routine

As described in the Post Workout Stretching

CHAPTER 24
WEEK 6

COACHING NOTES

This is it. You are nearly there. You are coming to the end of your 6 week training plan. You have most of the hard work done. The idea would be to run your target race at the end of this week. In doing so, we will do a slight taper this week. Tapering is where we let our bodies recover, a little more than normal, before a race. So this week will only be 3 sessions. There will be no hard session, apart from your 5k race.

You have to do two things on race day. Trust your training, and trust yourself. If you honestly put the work in, there is no reason why you won't completely smash your target race. Running a personal record will sometimes mean having all of the external factors falling into place. These can be weather, the course, the other competitors, the time of day, your health on the day, and so on. But with the work you put in, there is no reason that you shouldn't get yourself a PR on the day. I am so proud of all the work you have done and can't wait to hear from you with your result. Please send me your comments after you run your target 5k here: https://achieverc.com/5k-improvement-plan-feedback. It would mean an awful lot to me as your coach.

Session 1 (Day 17) - Easy Run
  Main Session
  4 miles easy run
  Stretching Routine
  As described in the Post Workout Stretching

Session 2 (Day 18) - Easy Run
  Warm-up
  Slow jog - 5 minutes
  Main Session
  2 miles easy run
  Cool-Down
  Slow jog - 5 minutes
  Stretching Routine
  As described in the Post Workout Stretching

. . .

Session 3 (Day 19) - 5k Race Day
Warm up

Slow jog - 5-10 minutes (to be finished about 15 minutes before the start).

Dynamic Warm-up

To be finished about 5 minutes before the start. Do these near the start line to ensure you aren't rushing to get there. Keep the start as stress free as possible.

- Running in place - 20 seconds
- High Knees - 20 seconds
- Running in place - 20 seconds
- Heel flicks - 20 seconds
- Running in place - 20 seconds
- Straight Leg Kicks - 20 seconds
- Running in place - 20 seconds
- A - Skips - 20 seconds
- Running in place - 20 seconds
- Lunges - 10 (5 each leg)
- Running in place - 20 seconds

Main Session

Stay calm, focussed and visualize finishing the race with your target time on the clock. Believe that you can do it. You WILL do it!

5k Race Day. Put it all together and give it all you got.

Cool-Down

5 minutes - Slow jog

Stretching Routine

As described in the Post Workout Stretching

CHAPTER 25
CONGRATULATIONS

YOU'VE DONE IT!

If you enjoyed this program, **please leave a positive review of this book on Amazon or wherever you purchased it**. It is so important to coaches and authors who are producing quality work for distribution.

It is a great way for this book to be put in front of more people. I've enjoyed working with you and please look for more of my books and training programs by browsing https://aheartforrunning.com/product-category/books. You will find more advanced, easy to follow programs for hitting your future distance and speed goals. For now, bask in the greatness of what you just achieved. I am proud of you and you should be too!

WIN A FREE MONTH OF PERSONAL COACHING

How about getting some personal one-to-one coaching. I offer one free month of coaching to one reader of my books every single month. It's very easy to be in with a chance to win. Simply go to Amazon and post an honest review of this book. Then, in order to let me know it was you, click (or navigate to) https://jmruncoach.com/book-feedback and paste that same review along with your email address. That's it, you are in with a chance. I would love to work with you personally and see you hit your running goals.

ADDITIONAL RESOURCES

Next up is the Half Marathon and 10k Improvement book coming soon on Amazon. Browse them all on my Amazon author page.

If you are interested in learning more about the author or need some additional inspiration, my memoir A Heart for Running: How Running Saved My Life is available on Amazon.

I would very much like to hear from you with feedback. I am extremely interested in your results

**from either your first 10k or from your target 5k race.
Please reach out to me on one of the following links:**

Blog - https://achieverc.com

Facebook - https://www.face-
book.com/groups/achieverc

Instagram - https://instagram.com/achieverunningclub

Twitter - https://twitter.com/achieverunners

YouTube - https://youtube.com/@achieverunningclub

CHAPTER 26
WHAT'S NEXT

YOU'VE JUST OPENED the door to three times as many events as there was when you finished the 5k distance. There are 5k, 5 miler, 10k events to be found throughout the year. You will start seeing the same faces over and over and get to know some of these people. This running community, that you now belong to, will be your friends for life. The shared experiences and mutual respect is the bond that holds this great family together. Congratulations on doing what you set out to do. I sincerely hope to see you posting your success stories on our Facebook group. Be part of the support and encouragement for all our runners, no matter what level. We are there to answer questions and concerns for everyone.

Look out for more books when you are ready to take on the half marathon, or even a full marathon. I will also have more advanced 5k and 10k plans to ensure your race times plummet to all time lows! Here's to many years of personal records.

ALSO BY JOHN MCDONNELL

A Heart for Running: How Running Saved My Life

Running for Beginners: The Easiest Guide to Running Your First 5K In Only 6 Weeks

Marathon Training Strategies: A Comprehensive Guide to Running Your Best Marathon - Including Plans, Advice, and Goal-Hitting Tips

APPENDIX I - BODYWEIGHT WORKOUT

Strength and conditioning training can be incredibly beneficial for runners, as it can help improve your performance, prevent injuries, and enhance your overall fitness. It does this in many ways and here are just a few of the benefits that are relevant to our goals as 10k runners:

1 Improved running economy: Strength and conditioning training can help runners improve your running economy, which is the amount of oxygen you consume while running at a certain pace. By improving your overall strength and endurance, you will become more efficient and use less energy to cover the same distance. This can lead to improved performance and faster race times. It will make easy runs feel easier and faster runs more achievable.

2 Injury prevention: Strength and conditioning training can help prevent common running injuries, such as IT band syndrome, shin splints, and plantar fasciitis. Strengthening the muscles around the knees, hips, and ankles will improve stability and reduce the risk of injury. Additionally, strength and conditioning training can help correct muscle imbalances, which can be a contributing factor to injuries.

3 Improved muscular endurance: Running long distances can be taxing on the muscles, and strength and conditioning training can help improve muscular endurance. By training the muscles to work harder for longer periods of time, you will improve your ability to maintain a consistent pace throughout a race or training run.

4 Increased bone density: Running is a weight-bearing activity, which can help improve bone density. However, strength and conditioning training can further enhance bone density, through the use of resistance. This can help reduce the risk of osteoporosis and other bone-related conditions.

Incorporating strength and conditioning training into your training plan will be beneficial in improving performance, preventing injuries, and enhancing overall fitness. I have included this bodyweight program which you will find both challenging, yet surprisingly achievable. I believe this workout is so effective because it is short enough to be non-intimidating, yet hard enough to cause adaptation over time. The key, like so many other things in sport, is consistency.

This will make the overall program that much easier to complete. For the first four weeks, limit this to 10 minutes per session, every day if possible. Do each of these for the number of repetitions (reps) or minutes per exercise until 10 minutes is up. In weeks five through eight, you should aim to do this same workout for 20 minutes, just looping through the workout until you hit 20 minutes.

10 x Push-ups

(if standard push-ups are too difficult, start by doing them from your knees)

20 x Crunches

Plank - 30 seconds

20 Squats

10 Dead Bugs

20 Lunges

If at any point this feels too easy, by all means, do more reps or more sets. Good technique is important in order to get the best results. You will be better off doing fewer reps with good technique and building up the quantity of reps over the weeks.

Demonstrations of these exercises can be found on my YouTube Channel: https://youtube.com/@aheartforrunning

Printed in Great Britain
by Amazon

40790417R00066